Small, yet Mighty

by Amanda Lee

illustrations by Lorryn Trujillo

This book is dedicated to Quintin,

my Small, yet Mighty little boy

who is forever my inspiration.

Library of Congress Cataloging-in-Publication Data has been applied for
ISBN: 978-0-578-36417-9

Illustrations by Lorryn Trujillo
Layout design by Pfeifer Design

Published by Amanda Lee

FORWARD

Small, yet Mighty is a nonfiction story about my then two-year-old son, Quintin, diagnosed with ASD. ASD or Atrial Septal Defect is a condition where a hole exists in the wall that separates the heart's chambers, an actual hole in the heart. With this defect, my young child experienced cyanotic episodes where he would turn blue from lack of oxygen in the blood pumped from his heart. So, after many visits to some of the best pediatric cardiologists, it was decided that Quintin would need open-heart surgery to repair the hole. However, it wasn't until after the surgery the doctors informed me that the right chamber was 4 times the size of the left chamber because it had to work extra hard to pump the blood, only confirming the surgery was the right choice for Quintin.

Before his surgery, I searched high and low for a book I could read with him to prepare him for the journey ahead. The process frightened me too, but I needed to calm his fears and make him as comfortable as possible as his mom. But I never found any age-appropriate books about a child facing surgery. So, I wrote a story and read it to him daily. During our time in Boston, the doctors and nurses were impressed and said they would buy the book if I published it. The rest is history!

As a parent, one of the hardest things is to see your child, especially one so young and vulnerable, go through any operation, let alone prepare them for it. I hope this book gives parents a go-to read to comfort them and their children. It doesn't just apply to those with Quintin's condition, but for any child about to have or experiencing surgery for many reasons.

Amanda Lee

Quintin is a happy and adventurous
little two-year-old boy.

He loves to run and play and climb
as any toddler does.

But when Quintin was three months old, the doctors found he was born with a hole in his heart. The hole was large enough that the healthy side of his heart had to work extra hard.

The doctors decided Quintin needed
surgery to stitch up the one-inch hole,
so his heart didn't have to
work extra hard.

Quintin's family traveled to the
best doctors and nurses in a fancy,
busy city known as Boston.

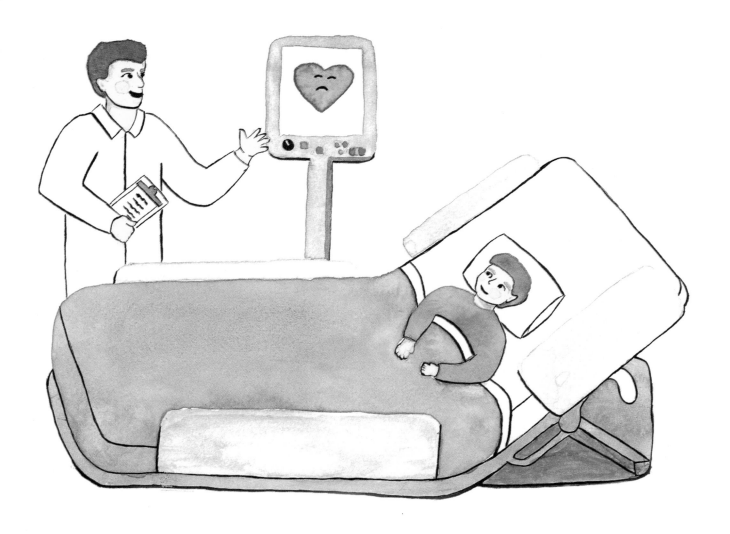

Quintin had hours of testing with X-ray machines and other big scary-looking equipment the day before surgery.

Then Quintin met a little girl named
Ava-Lynn. She also had a hole in her heart
and was having the same surgery.

On the day of his surgery, Quintin had to
wait a long time until it was his turn.
This was hard because he was not
allowed to eat before the surgery.

Quintin was a brave boy when the doctors gave him a ride in a push car to the operating room.

When it was over, Quintin's mom and dad were taken to a special place in the hospital called the ICU. This was where they saw Quintin sleeping in his special bed.

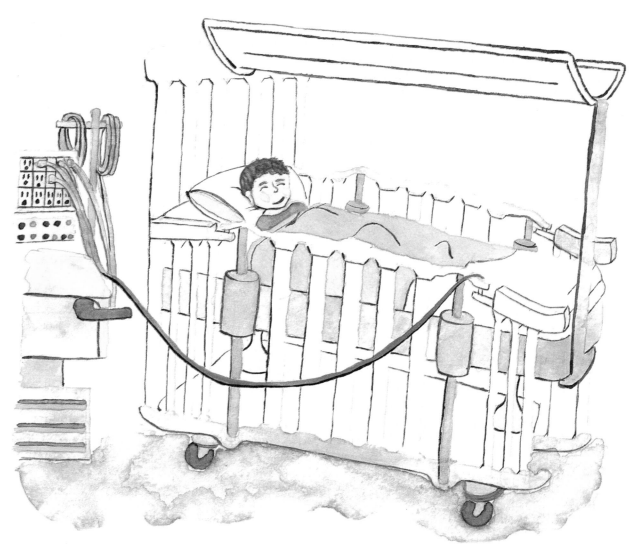

There were many cords, wires, and tubes doing different jobs to make him feel as comfortable as possible.

Within hours of his surgery, Quintin woke up and wanted to move. Mom helped him to the floor, and he took a couple steps. It was hard and hurt a little.

The hospital had a red wagon so Quintin
could take a ride around the ICU.
The nurses gave him a purple pop and
lots of special toys.

Quintin stayed in the ICU for one night and then moved to the children's cardiology recovery floor. This floor had two toy rooms, lots of fun toys, and other wonderful gifts.

Quintin became very fond of one nurse named Sydney. He always bounced up when she walked into the room.

Quintin found his friend, Ava-Lynn, and
her family. She was just a couple rooms
down from him.

Quintin and Ava-Lynn enjoyed
being pushed in the cars
around the hospital.

These cars helped Quintin because he still had chest tubes in, and he would get tired. But every day, Quintin grew stronger.

Once the chest tubes came out,
he was UNSTOPPABLE.

He was a small yet mighty Quintin.

EPILOGUE

In Quintin's little life so far, he has had a total of three surgeries. The most significant was the open-heart surgery and the other two for ear tube placements. And each time, he has just grown stronger. Thankfully, Quintin has had zero cyanotic episodes since his heart surgery and is now considered average height and weight.

After all Quintin went through, there is nothing sweeter than watching him run and jump and play like every other child his age! Quintin has blessed me with his smile, enthusiasm for life, and his strength. I know he won't be small for long, but he will always be mighty!

2 years after his surgery

ABOUT THE AUTHOR

My first job is being the mother of two boys, Elijah and Quintin. My second job is being a special educator in a local elementary school. It is cliche to say, but I feel completely blessed with the jobs I always dreamt of achieving. I have a passion for children's education and growth. And now, sharing Quintin's experience to help others understand what to expect, and know it will be okay, gives me a further sense of pride.

Made in the USA
Columbia, SC
29 March 2022

58231187R00015